GOING UNDERGROUND
BIRMINGHAM

ANTHONY POULTON-SMITH

AMBERLEY

First published 2022

Amberley Publishing, The Hill, Stroud
Gloucestershire GL5 4EP

www.amberley-books.com

British Library Cataloguing in Publication Data.
A catalogue record for this book is available from the British Library.

ISBN 978 1 3981 0179 1 (print)
ISBN 978 1 3981 0180 7 (ebook)

Typesetting by SJmagic DESIGN SERVICES, India.
Printed in the UK.

CONTENTS

1

BENEATH OUR FEET

Birmingham's 1.2 million inhabitants give the place the status as the 'Second City'. Located close to the geographical centre of England, it is the focal point for the nation's transport system. Rightly claiming it has more miles of canal than Venice, the city is also a busy railway hub and near where several motorways connect. Be it on water, rail or road, the traffic, at some point, finds itself below ground level as it passes through the city.

Like many cities Birmingham's earlier days often lie buried beneath more recent constructions. A market town since the middle of the thirteenth century, by the beginning of the sixteenth century the population had reached just 1,500, exceeding 10,000 two centuries later. Now the growth began to accelerate, over succeeding centuries hitting 73,000 in 1800, and over half a million by 1901. Styled 'the City of 1,000 Trades', unlike other centres of industry to the north it did not rely largely on one industry, such as wool and cotton. Birmingham's industrial strength was its diversity, built on adaptability and creativity with a well-paid and highly skilled workforce.

Clearly the city's growth is largely restricted to the last two centuries. While this is true of most urban centres, no city in the United Kingdom has seen such a rapid expansion over a similar period. Yet this does not mean any less can be found under Birmingham. Very few will have seen what exists beneath more than 100 square miles of the city. Likely the most any of us have seen is by peering into the hole opened to allow maintenance, be it telephone, cable, power lines, gas and water pipes, or sewage. Some will have travelled, on boats or on foot, through the tunnels cut by canal builders more than two centuries ago. Many more will have travelled tunnels bringing railways from the nineteenth century. Yet little can be seen on a boat or train, while spatial awareness is a mystery.

Beneath all our towns and cities are buried an astonishing array of cables and pipes. Each facilitate a service we often take for granted and hardly consider until that service fails. A cross-section of almost any ordinary town centre street will come as a surprise. One of the most common sights for us are the drains. Metal grills at the side of the road take water from the gutters and takes it – we will see later. Necessarily open to the sky to permit water to drain makes these most familiar for us. But we can only see a small opening, and depth perception is difficult. Legislation defines the maximum and minimum depths of drainage systems as between 75 cm and 135 cm below the finished ground level. Note this is not the natural level but the finished level after construction and also refers to the topmost point, meaning the low point is rather deeper. These depths are not chosen arbitrarily. A minimum of 75 cm ensures protection from frost under normal conditions in the United Kingdom – although 'normal' can differ widely in terms of location and altitude. But a maximum of 135 cm also allows reasonable access for repairs and/or maintenance.

Surface water drains are initially shallow and drain away in one of three ways. It is not desirable to direct this into sewers with so-called foul water if possible. For quite isolated properties the surface water is likely drained to a soakaway adjacent to, or quite near, the property. Alternatively, there may be a dedicated surface water sewer, often referred to as a stormwater drain, which probably empties into a nearby watercourse. Finally, surface water can be directed into the sewer, along with the foul water, although technically a sewer is only referred to as such when it serves more than one property, otherwise it is merely a drain. It is easy to see how confusion exists when a sewer can sometimes be a drain and vice versa, and that does not take into consideration the complexity of sewerage laws.

We should also look at the different ways sewage is moved along and where it ends up. Some remote locations will utilise a septic tank or sludge tank. However, the vast majority is taken to sewage farms where it is treated and separated into clean water and recyclable organic products. Water heads to the river system, nature's drains, the reclaimed organic matter used for fertilisers. Unfortunately, other items also find a way into the sewage farms. Be they washed down drains after being discarded thoughtlessly instead of using many waste bins provided, or wrongly flushed down a toilet, they are retrieved, separated and dealt with elsewhere. There are very good reasons why we are told not to put oil-based products down a drain or flush anything other than toilet paper – and, of course, what that paper is designed to clean up.

Sewage movement uses the simplest of technologies, the force of gravity through the medium of liquid water. Next time you ascend that steep hill, glad to reach the summit when at least a little out of breath, look back and think about what is happening underground. Imagine what would happen if the load of sewage contained in that drop could be seen above street level. It would all be at the foot of the slope. If that happened underground the system would soon be blocked and so a series of steps create waterfalls and deliver its contents to the bottom of the slope in a manageable volume. Little and nothing can go wrong with this system. Hence if the road has been dug up for repair to the sewer it is likely the problem is caused by incorrect use of the system.

Perhaps one of the most common problems in modern sewage systems are those known as 'fatbergs'. These clumps of non-biodegradable matter (i.e. that which should not be in the sewers), form out of sight and build to such a size they will easily block the sewer. In London in 2018, a fatberg was discovered in a sewer comprised of congealed fat from kitchens, wet wipes, disposable nappies, machine oil, and condoms. It took nine weeks to restore the sewer to a working condition. Nine weeks to clear just 250 metres of sewer, a little at a time, until all 130 tons of this 'toxic monster' had been removed. This shows the dimensions of the sewers beneath our feet.

Generally, sewers are rather smaller than the London home of the Whitechapel Fatberg. These can be quite shallow in some places but normally sewage pipes will be almost 2 metres below ground. This helps prevent problems caused by sub-zero temperatures – a frozen river of biodegradable sewage would soon cause appalling problems for the world above. Not least the noxious odours.

When school chums pointed out 'stinkpipes' or 'stenchpoles' on the way to and from school, they would add how these were to remove the smell from the sewers. Their stories were half right. They are linked to the sewers but exist more to allow the escape of methane, a potentially explosive gas which is a by-product of the sewage breaking down. Statistics for Birmingham are very difficult to quantify, for the city covers 267.8 square km and authorities are very aware not all water mains and sewers are recorded. However, we can offer a conservative estimate of at least 500 kilometres of water mains and 350 kilometres of sewers within the city's boundaries.

Not only water and sewage are found in underground pipes. While some houses today are all-electric, once gas was the only source of power into domestic properties. Not, as we would think, for cooking and heating, most often cooking was done on the range and heating by coal fires, but for lighting. As with water supplies, gas came through a main pipe to an area and then tapped to individual houses. Legislation demands a gas main be buried a minimum of 75 cm under a road or verge and 60 cm under a footpath. Service pipes to each property should have a minimum depth of 37.5 cm on private ground and 45 cm under footpaths and highways.

Anyone who has stood alongside a hole where excavations have revealed gas mains will be aware the visible pipe is well below 75 cm deep. This is also the case with water and sewers, both of which are much older than cables laid for electricity, for television, or the internet. Do not think this shows previous generations were willing to bury the pipes lower. Indeed, the reverse is true and the reason the pipes are deeper down is because street level is higher than ever. It is natural to build on top of earlier constructions and as archaeologists will tell you, the deeper you dig the further back in time you get.

Clearly cable television and internet services are little more than a generation old. As already noted, electricity supplies are much more recent – the second city not having access to any electricity supply until 1903, although many stuck with gas lamps until much later. Interestingly, and an indication of the fragmented supply in the early days, while the Midland Electricity Company had their offices in Temple Street, this company did not supply Birmingham. That came from the City of Birmingham Electricity Supply Department and the Summer Lane Power Station. Cables are much easier to damage than pipes and should be enclosed in a conduit for added protection. For ease of recognition, all cables are coded, using coloured cable, tape, warning devices, marks and any number of other forms of identification.

Under roads and pavements, such should be a minimum of 60 cm beneath the surface, although on private property this changes to 45 cm for driveways, 15 cm beneath soil or grass, and 10 cm beneath concrete or paving. Note the recommended depth for flower beds is usually given as two spade depths as they are likely to be dug over.

It is safe to assume the length of cable and pipe for gas, electricity, and internet and/ or television are each at least comparable to that of the fresh water supplies. In truth the internet will certainly be rather less but electricity, owing to the street lighting and traffic signals, will be much greater. Thus, we can add another 1,500 kilometres to the 850 kilometres for water and sewage. This total, 2,350 kilometres, is approximately the distance from Birmingham to Bucharest.

With all this beneath our towns and cities, we tend to take these utilities for granted. Indeed, we hardly consider what lies there until they fail to work and then roads are dug up to correct the problem. This is when we hear how this street or that road is up again! Note this only applies where streets are at close to land level, that of the natural topography. For those areas developed after years of mining or quarrying, depths are far greater.

We have still to address the subterranean passages used by canal boats, natural waterways, and railway tunnels. Then we have basements, both modern and old, used and abandoned, hidden, forgotten and even, on some occasions, still utilised. And we must not forget the archaeology. While not technically accessible, which probably prevents any

The tunnel near Moseley station.

suggestion they are 'underground' and should be considered 'buried', they do warrant at least a brief look.

In the following pages something of the hidden world beneath the ground will be revealed. All manner of surprising discoveries unearthed: some well known or predictable, others long buried, forgotten or previously unknown.

2

DWARF HOLES

What lies beneath Birmingham will include looks at canals, railways and roads. For our first example, we need to look under and alongside all three. Nationally the so-called Spaghetti Junction may just be the city's most famous image. Correctly known as the Gravelly Hill Interchange, we begin at the highest point, where the elevated section of the M6 and the A38M Aston Expressway carry an average of over 200,000 vehicles every single day.

Those on the motorway will be oblivious of what lies beneath unless they leave the motorway network via the slip road. Exits take motorists to another road network, comprised of Gravelly Hill Road, Tyburn Road, Lichfield Road, Minstead Road, Copeley Hill and Slade Road. Together with the motorway access points these combine in a traffic island known as Salford Circus. Other levels are found under the area, but it is the name 'Salford' that interests us for this is the clue to earlier times. We shall return to look at that name shortly.

First comes the next level, for this is also where the cross-city line from Lichfield heads to Birmingham New Street. Looping around the north of Salford Circus between stations at Gravelly Hill and Aston, built by the London & North Western Railway in 1862 and known as the Sutton Coldfield Branch, it occupies the same route it did over 150 years ago. Electrified in 1978, it is part of the ever-improving 50 miles of the Cross-City Line and has certainly seen many changes since the first locomotive ever connected with the Grand Junction Railway at Aston.

Other travel routes meeting here are the canals. Three man-made navigable waterways converge on this same point at Salford Circus: the Tame Valley Canal from the north-west opened in 1844, Birmingham and Fazeley Canal from the east completed in 1789, and from the south the Birmingham and Warwick Junction Canal, which, since 1929, has been considered part of the Grand Union Canal.

Built many years before the railway, but not prior to the canal, the record of Salford Bridge from 1883 is most interesting. This record speaks of the bridge as the (then) contemporary crossing, going on to refer to an earlier forded crossing (as the name of Salford suggests) further upstream. This was found about 50 metres upstream from that bridge and where Hawthorne Brook once joined the River Tame. This confluence was described as 'gravelly', making it sufficient to support the wheel of a cart. Note, too, the description of 'gravelly', itself the reason Gravelly Hill is named. While the Tame is clearly visible, Hawthorne Brook runs through an underground culvert for all but a very short distance before joining the Tame. This visible from the Tame Valley Canal towpath but almost indistinguishable as a separate watercourse.

Above: Somewhere under the vegetation the Hawthorne Brook joins the River Tame…

Below: …in the shadow of Spaghetti Junction.

Not only does the name of Salford tell of the former river crossing, the original form reveals more. Scaford or Scraford takes its first element from *scraet* or *scrat*. The true meaning of this word is not overly clear and, quite possibly, not particularly relevant. For obvious reasons it has been said to mean 'secret' or 'scratch', less obviously 'cave'. This last definition is only used when referring to another facet of this site: the Dwarf Holes. The term was certainly in use by the very early seventeenth century, for there is a record of Dwarfehole Mill. While 'dwarf' has just one meaning today, earlier many euphemisms existed in reference to the devil – these included 'goblin' and 'dwarf'.

Sandstone Cliff at Tyburn Road, Salford Circus.

Dwarf Holes referred to caves in the sandstone at what is now Salford Circus. Some records state these were caves once inhabited by early humans during the Stone Age and only uncovered when rediscovered by Victorian children – fanciful thinking at best. The caves were certainly well known, appearing on several maps since the seventeenth century, and certainly did not date from the Neolithic. Eroded into the sandstone at the foot of Copeley Hill by either the River Tame or Hawthorne Brook, there was some indication these were enlarged by hand, perhaps even entirely man-made. They were utilised as bomb shelters during the Second World War.

Something of the sandstone cliff remains, seen on the Tyburn Road exit from Salford Circus. However, the Dwarf Holes were destroyed with the building of the Gravelly Hill Interchange, work beginning in 1968 and opening on 24 May 1972.

Benjamin Stone's image of the so-called Dwarf Holes on Tyburn Road.

3

SNOW HILL TO MOOR STREET

With the many lines through Birmingham New Street station, there will always be numerous tunnels and stories to tell, but one which does not link to New Street station deserves a special mention. Today the city centre has three stations: New Street, Snowhill and Moor Street.

Moor Street station opened in 1909, a Great Western Railway station with services to Leamington Spa and Stratford-upon-Avon, services which still operate from there today. Snow Hill station, also on the Great Western Railway, opened in 1852 and at its height rivalled New Street with services to London, Liverpool, Wales, and the south-west. A 580-metre tunnel linked Moor Street to Snow Hill but, this officially closed on 4 March 1968, two days after the last train used it, and Snow Hill saw its last passenger exactly four years later. In 1977 Snow Hill was demolished and became a car park.

Moor Street to Snow Hill Tunnel. (Courtesy of Geoff Dowling)

Plans to rebuild Snow Hill and relocate Moor Street, including reopening the tunnel, came in the 1980s. The new station is more functional than its predecessor, a slight realignment at Moor Street enabled the former third track to be extended through Snow Hill Tunnel. On 5 October 1987, the new Snow Hill Station opened, the same day as the Snow Hill Tunnel and today millions pass through the tunnel beneath the Second City each year.

However, the excitement came prior to opening. When plans to reopen the tunnel were approved and the tunnel cleared, an audacious and outstanding opportunity was offered. For a donation to charity anyone would be allowed to walk the tunnel. On Sunday 18 March 1987, a queue formed and snaked around what was then the inner ring road as an astonishing 13,000 people arrived for a unique experience. It may come as a surprise to discover the tunnel was created using the cut and cover method as far as Temple Row. Thereafter a deep cutting ran to Snow Hill station, with a clue as to what lies beneath in the name of the famous Great Western Arcade, which runs above the line of the track.

The tunnel leading from Moor Street station to Snow Hill station.

4

BANK OF ENGLAND

As everyone knows the Bank of England is in London. Since its founding in 1694, and its move to Threadneedle Street in 1734, it has not only been the model for most central banks across the world but symbolises Britain. But in Birmingham?

In 1829 the joint-stock bank was established by private bankers Gibbins & Lovell. Originally known as the Birmingham Banking Company, its rapid rise saw it move from headquarters in New Street to the junction of Bennetts Hill and Waterloo Street in 1831. The latter building was added to in 1868 and extended from 1881. Despite the financial crisis of 1866, when the bank failed with assets of just £280,000 and liabilities of £1.8 million (equal to 100 times that today), it soon recovered and prospered as the Metropolitan Bank until acquired by the Midland Bank in 1914. Former headquarters on the corner of Waterloo Street still shows the name of the Midland Bank in its façade, although the branch closed in 2002 and is now a popular public house.

As indicated in the previous chapter, a tunnel ran between Snow Hill and Moor Street, but there was a side tunnel and a line turning off and running to one of the banks in New Street. Here cash could be transported in safety away from nefarious eyes.

Below street level a track still exists, although it no longer goes anywhere.

5

NEW STREET STATION

With almost 50 million passengers annually, this is by far the largest of Birmingham's railway stations. Indeed, New Street station serves more passengers than every other station across the city combined.

Built over eight years from 1846 in an area known for its marshes, it slowly replaced several termini, which, thus far, had brought passengers only to the outskirts of the city centre. Most notable of these was Curzon Street, now planned as the terminus for the new HS2 rail system. Naming the 3-acre site New Street station could be seen as a misnomer, for it not only replaced seventy houses and the Countess of Huntingdon's Connexion Chapel (only built six years earlier) but erased Peck Lane, The Froggary, Queen Street and Colmore Street from the map. In their place a station now boasting the world's largest single-span arched roof.

This region had previously been known as a Jewish quarter. It is this which may have led to the ghost stories that speak of an old corridor with white tiling cutting through a Jewish cemetery, those buried there unable to rest and said to be haunting the area. The corridor had a curve, meaning it was impossible to see along it and this may have also contributed to the stories. As far as we are aware while the tiled passage still exists, the cemetery never has.

Little changed until the 1960s, when it was completely rebuilt to produce an enclosed station with buildings over most of what was the old span. Thirteen platforms now doubled passenger numbers using the station but did not prove popular with Brummies, who missed the Victorian splendour. Further development completed in 2015 cost £550 million, with the West Midlands Metro tram line extension from Snow Hill opening the following May.

Travelling on the lines to New Street, where light levels permit, reveals the work in the 1960s. Clearly these are former cuttings, now covered by buildings.

6

THE MAILBOX

One line you will not see today at New Street station is that which once ran to the Mailbox. Since 1997 the building is associated with shops and offices, yet previously it had been the largest automated parcels and letters sorting office in the United Kingdom.

Built in 1970, this former railway goods yard and the canal wharves of the Birmingham and Worcester Canal brought most of its mail underground. An electric tractor hauled carts loaded with sacks of mail to and from New Street station. The tunnel still exists and emerges at platform 6. When illuminated it is easy to see the undulations of this almost straight tunnel.

Although the last mail sack ran along here in 1997, the tunnel is remarkably clean. There are some reminders of the past at the Mailbox end. A sign warns drivers to keep the speed down, and barriers ensure the loading area is separate from the route used by the

Mailbox Tunnel looking towards New Street station...

vehicles. Some evidence of current use, mainly by maintenance staff, at the south-east end is markedly different to what is found at New Street station.

A grid prevents access to the station, now permanently fixed to prevent station staff wheeling large rubbish bins further along the tunnel. Aside from the daylight, the sound of trains and announcements leave no doubt as to what lies beyond.

Above: …and emerging from the tunnel at the sorting office.

Left: Where the mail was sorted – note the warning to drivers to stop.

7

ODEON NEW STREET

Before we leave New Street, we should pay a visit to the local cinema. What is now the Odeon New Street opened on 4 September 1937 as a Paramount Cinema, built on the site of the former King Edward's School, then one of just seven Paramount cinemas in cities around the United Kingdom. Filmgoers flocked to see Errol Flynn in *The Charge of the Light Brigade* on that Saturday – most of the 2,439 seats occupied. The cinema became the Odeon in 1941, a chain founded by Birmingham-born Oscar Deutsch a decade earlier.

Then a single auditorium, the Odeon New Street played host to many of the most famous acts of the day. The Beatles played here in October 1965, the Rolling Stones in September 1973, and Iron Maiden in the 1980s. Other acts include the Everly Brothers, Mickie Most, the Shirelles, Eric Burdon, Gene Vincent, Duane Eddy, and a rather disgruntled Bob Dylan who complained about working on a dirty stage!

In April 1965, the cinema closed for modernisation. Out went the old art deco style and in came the new streamlined and featureless design. When reopening on 24 June 1965, the audience were treated to a showing of *Genghis Khan* starring Omar Sharif, together with a thirty-minute set from Cliff Richard and the Shadows. Surely as odd a programme ever seen either here or anywhere in the city.

Odeon New Street underground screen.

In May 1988, a second closure for refurbishment resulted in an even more featureless design opening in August 1988, when this became a six-screen cinema. In 1991 the original Compton organ from the Paramount days was dismantled and sold. Two extra screens were also installed at this time, one replacing the bar in the basement, which is still open today. All eight screens now cater for a total audience of 1,268.

Odeon New Street and, for a multiscreen cinema, not a very tall building is a clue.

8

ABC NEW STREET

As if New Street did not have enough beneath it already, there was once another cinema. Indeed, this is the oldest of them all. Built as a Masonic Hall, the first films were shown here in 1896, just weeks after the first ever movie shown in the United Kingdom. Converted to a full-time cinema in July 1910, when it was known as the Theatre de Luxe, it became the Regent Cinema in 1922, the Forum Cinema in 1930, and ABC in 1961.

The former ABC New Street above ground.

The narrow New Street entrance contrasted with a grand interior. Seating 1,259 – 501 stalls, 348 in the circle, with 410 in a very steep upper circle – early showings are not known. However, we do know the Forum opened to a double bill of *Loose Ends* and *Kiss Me Sergeant*. Like most cinemas of the time it had an organ. This removed in 1955.

The last reel shown here, on 9 April 1983, was Stephen Spielberg's *ET: the Extra-Terrestrial*. The frontage then became an amusement arcade, with the remainder given over to retail. Today the ground floor is home to a restaurant and take away. From outside, the exterior newly and tastefully repainted, the building blends in well, a good modern look on an impressive building of architectural delights from yesteryear.

Signs of its earlier use can still be found. In the basement the original cloakrooms and fire exits are, we are confidently advised, still in place. Meanwhile the upper storeys still house the auditorium, albeit it is difficult to see it as such today. This cavernous area has air conditioning ducts, serving the food outlets below, looping around giving the whole place a most eerie feel.

Underneath the ABC New Street today.

9

ODEON QUEENSWAY

And before we leave cinemas there is a third underground screen in the 'Second City'. Odeon Queensway is possibly the lost cinema Brummies remember most fondly. Situated 12 metres underneath Scala House, it was originally known as Scala Theatre.

It closed for refurbishment before reopening in November 1964 as Scala Superama. In 1970 it became part of the Odeon group, first known as Odeon Ringway and, two years on, Odeon Queensway. A further change in the late seventies saw two additional screens, each of 115 seats, complimenting the 555-seat main auditorium (they also allowed forty to stand). Small auditoria with small screens, but state-of-the-art sound accompanying 70 mm projection. Such a small cinema would never be the financial draw of Odeon New Street and its multi-screens. Odeon Queensway closed its doors for the last time in September 1988.

Today the cinema still exists locked away beneath Scala House. While the terraced seating area is still obvious, it was emptied of chairs years ago. As with most abandoned underground areas, water has taken its toll. A few 'Odeon' signs heaped to one side are the only link to the past.

10

QUEENSWAY TUNNELS

Access to the Odeon Queensway was through the underpass at what is today referred to as Pagoda Island. We will look deeper into Birmingham's underpasses in subsequent chapters. Here, suffice to say, these tunnels allowed pedestrians to 'cross the road' in safety. Pagoda Island does still permit access between Holloway Head, Smallbrook Queensway, Horse Fair, and Bristol Street via a series of puffin crossings.

Left: Approaching Pagoda Island underpass from the south.

Below: And Pagoda Island's underpass from the north.

Looking towards the northern
entrance to Queensway Tunnel.

Yet underground access is still available here, albeit only for motorists. Beneath our feet
traffic is carried by the A38 trunk road, one of the city's busiest arterial roads. This is the
southernmost and shortest of three dips of this trunk road in less than a mile. All three
constitute part of the A4400 Inner Ring Road, constructed from the 1960s.

Right: Passing through
Queensway Tunnel.

Below: Queensway
Tunnel.

North of here is the longest underground section. Officially named the Queensway Tunnel, it was opened in January 1971 by Queen Elizabeth II and Duke of Edinburgh. In her opening speech the queen spoke of the project being completed six years ahead of schedule, also inadvertently naming the whole route 'Queensway' instead of just that from Great Charles Street. Several buildings disappeared forever to make way, including Birmingham Reference Library, the Birmingham and Midlands Institute, Birmingham Conservatoire, and Bishop's Palace. St Chad's Cathedral, which we will encounter in the next chapter, was only saved by a single vote at the council meeting. This resulted in the rather twisting route of a comparatively short tunnel.

At 548 metres it ranks among the twenty longest road tunnels in the United Kingdom. In 2013 plans to link the Queensway and St Chad's Tunnels into a single tunnel were voiced but gained little support. These came a year after suggestions of closing the 170-metre St Chad's Tunnel to smash Birmingham's the so-called 'concrete collar' and open it up as a pedestrian boulevard. Neither plan came to fruition and since a series of closures and refurbishments of both tunnels are presumably an indication that these tunnels, now fifty years old, are likely to remain for many years to come.

Left: Emerging from the Queensway Tunnel.

Below: Inside St Chad's underpass.

11

ST CHAD'S CATHEDRAL

As we have already passed St Chad's Cathedral, this seems the best time to cover the underground crypt. Built in three years from 1838 and dedicated to St Chad of Mercia, this was the first Catholic church to be built in the country since the English Reformation in the sixteenth century. Opening in 1841, it was raised to cathedral status eleven years later. The architect was Augustus Welby Pugin, pioneer of the Gothic Revival style evident throughout.

An impressive site but beneath lies an even more impressive crypt.

Siting in the Gun Quarter brought it into danger during the Second World War. Indeed, on 22 November 1940 an incendiary device came through the roof of the south aisle. The bomb bounced and broke central heating pipes nearby. Water poured from the heating system dousing the flames and a thanksgiving tablet now marks the event: 'Deo Gratias 22 Nov 1940' ('Thanks be to God').

The first Bishop of Birmingham, William Bernard Ullathorne OS, died in 1911 and is buried at St Dominic's Priory, Stone, Staffordshire. Yet in the cathedral's crypt is a monument to Bishop Ullathorne.

Today it is difficult to see the area around St Chad's through modern development. This place of worship is built on a remarkably steep slope. Visitors are surprised to discover such a large crypt, which helped Pugin virtually embed the building deeper into the slope. Today the last resting place for families in their tombs and former cathedral clergy, it also houses a collection of medieval carvings and is where the choir practice. In the crypt it is easy to hear the four lanes of traffic running through the adjacent tunnel.

12

STEELHOUSE LANE POLICE STATION AND THE LAW COURTS

Steelhouse Lane police station was opened in 1933. Built on the same site as the earlier Victorian station, it is no accident the building backs on to the rear of the former Victoria Law Courts. Its predecessor hosted the first ever rehearsal by the City of Birmingham Orchestra (now the City of Birmingham Symphony Orchestra) on 4 September 1920. We can only wonder what any prisoners thought of the music at 9.30 in the morning!

Guests awaiting Her Majesty's pleasure would have been happier to see the station had its own bar, albeit only serving off-duty officers. This called time for the final time in 2005. Prisoners would only be held here for a maximum of twenty-four hours, awaiting their court appearance the day after their arrest. Those arrested elsewhere in the city would be brought here by van on the morning of their court appearance.

When the police station closed on 15 January 2017, there were calls to open the Steelhouse Lane Lock Up as a museum. Today open days are arranged for visitors. Hopefully this will result in more regular opening. Visitors can see a tunnel, albeit only through the viewing panel in the door from the lock-up. Running under Coleridge Passage, it allows passage between the police station and the courts. It had three functions: to prevent escape, to prevent the public from attacking the prisoners, and to prevent supporters of the prisoners from attacking the police.

The corridor between the police station in Steelhouse Lane and the law courts.

The tunnel was included in the original station and utilised in the rebuild, albeit the original floor had been lower. This lower floor level may explain why a police officer, in the tunnel to access the offices and documents on the court side, saw a figure ahead of him who, when they turned the corner, appeared to be just 4 feet tall and quickly vanished.

Among those who have walked the tunnel are Harry Fowler, Ernest Bayles, Stephen McHickie and Thomas Gilbert, doing so in October 1904. These four are the inspiration for the families featured by Steven Knight in the BAFTA award-winning series *Peaky Blinders*. Mug shots of the four men, all wearing their trademark flat caps, adorn the walls of the lock-up. Others to have walked the tunnel prior to the First World War were twenty-seven-year-old prostitute Gertrude Myers; fifteen-year-old housebreaker Winnie Moorcroft; William Gordon, arrested for being drunk and disorderly; and Thomas McDermott for robbing a warehouse. In more recent years famous 'guests' have included mass-murderer Fred West and the so-called Birmingham Six.

For years, the existence of the tiled tunnel was thought the stuff of legends. Now visitors to the lock-up can see it through the viewing panel. Open for 125 years, the tunnel would have seen innumerable prisoners, likely every individual facing a murder charge. We can only wonder how many prisoners were set free, never to return along the tunnel. And how many walked back to the holding cells, later taken to a prison, possibly to await execution.

Above: Coleridge Passage is said to run directly along the line of the underground passage from the police station to courts.

Left: The outside of the old police station in Steelhouse Lane.

13

UNDERGROUND RIVERS

Another police station houses a collection known as the West Midlands Police Museum. Adjacent to Sparkhill Library, it not only contained cells but had its own court. This is commemorated in the name of Court Road.

However, it is not Sparkhill's police station that intrigues us but the name of the district. A clue to its etymology is found in the name of the adjoining district of Sparkbrook, for there is a Spark Brook here. For at least part of the way Spark Brook marks the boundary between Sparkhill and Sparkbrook, its line above ground largely following that of Stoney Lane. On the corner with Highgate Road stood the Lamb and Flag public house. There are still those who recall having to bail out the flood water from the pub's cellars after prolonged rain, evidence of the nearby Spark Brook.

Spark Brook is joined by several tributaries before it meets the River Cole, all of which are culverted for at least most if not all of their course. Our earliest records of the source of Spark Brook has it rising at Belle Walk near the junction with Stoney Lane. If this does mark its source, then it seems to be the run-off from a spring. That spring would likely be the same as that recorded as *Bullan Wellan* or 'the Bull's Spring', as a boundary mark in the Yardley Charter, a document dated AD 972.

It is possible to get a glimpse of the Spark Brook. Although largely culverted in 1896, it had become little more than an open sewer and proven a major health hazard, but it is possible to trace its path. As already mentioned, the brook follows the line of Stoney Lane until reaching the junction with Walford Road – this another boundary marker in the Yardley Charter and known as 'the tall oak' – and on towards Golden Hillock Road.

Near the source
of Spark Brook.

Here at the site of the former BSA factory, it is possible to see it before it descends into a tunnel and passes under the Grand Union Canal. From what little can be seen of Spark Brook it seems the waters, despite being covered, still suffer from pollution and run-off from the built-up areas through which it flows. Certainly, this is not the open sewer of the late nineteenth century, but it could certainly be much cleaner.

Perhaps the best known of Birmingham's rivers is the River Rea. There is even a street named for it in Digbeth. Rising at Windmill Hill in the Waseley Hills Country Park, it flows largely north-east to meet the River Tame almost under Spaghetti Junction. That it flows generally northward makes it unique as the only river in Birmingham to do so, the rest all flowing generally southward. Only 15 miles in length, it is joined by an impressive number of tributaries for a comparatively short river. Furthermore, many of these tributaries have names of their own, which is most surprising as most minor tributaries are nearly always considered part of the main river. Yet on Birmingham's maps we can trace the courses of tributaries known as Callow Brook, Merritts Brook, Griffins Brook, the Bourn, Bourn Brook, Bartley Brook, Chad Brook and Wood Brook. Together these eight tributaries more than double the length of the Rea.

Merrits Brook, a tributary of the Rea.

Many tributaries drained a significant area of the Birmingham plateau, hence when it rains the largely culverted Rea can rise rapidly. As someone who once worked in the basement in a factory alongside the culverted Rea, the author has first-hand experience of just how fast the waters can rise and, during the worst rains, entering the building's basement through a wall which clearly was not watertight.

The River Rea emerges into daylight.

The culverted Rea shortly before it disappears underground at Highgate.

Spending much of its time hidden, the river is exposed as it passes through the old Longbridge car factory's works. Once it flowed beneath the sprawling factory site, now the £2 million development of Austin Park has seen the Rea open to the light again, and for the first time in a century. Although some will have known of the river's existence, the project describes the river as 'rediscovered' rather than 'uncovered'. Yet it soon disappears below ground again at the site of the old pumping station.

At the junction of Pershore Road and Cartland Road the waters of the Bourn join, itself starting out as Merritts Brook and becoming the Bourn when joining Griffins Brook. After a long stretch in the open through Canon Hill Park and passing Warwickshire County Cricket Club, where it gives its name to one end, it largely vanishes from view. Finally, it emerges and is swallowed up by the Tame beneath the elevated section of the M6 motorway.

Although extremely difficult to quantify with any accuracy, of the 30 plus miles of the Rea and its tributaries it seems at some time almost a third of this length has, at some time, travelled underground. Even before pollution decimated the river's wildlife, a lack of sunlight will have isolated the various lengths of water. With all these difficulties, it is remarkable we see any plants and animals in and alongside the Rea.

The longest river flowing through Birmingham is the River Cole, although not all its 25 miles flows through the city's boundaries. Its few tributaries are short and carry little water. However, the system has boasted many watermills throughout recorded history, averaging at least one per mile. Interestingly no part of the Cole or its tributaries runs underground except for a very short stretch which formerly fed the mill race at Sarehole Mill. Once running under Brook Lane via a culvert, this is long blocked and the line of the race northward is no longer traceable.

The young River Rea.

Site of former mill race
culverted near Sarehole Mill.

14

SUBWAYS

Construction techniques in the post-war years improved to the point where developers were suggesting high-rise blocks to answer the problem of space to build. Councils also seemed to latch on to this idea of looking to answer difficulties vertically instead of horizontally as had been the case since time immemorial. Thus, instead of creating pedestrian crossing points at busy junctions, the answer came in the form of the subway.

It is difficult to estimate the amount of abandoned and now infilled subways under Birmingham. We have already mentioned those once enabling pedestrians to cross what is today known as the Pagoda Island. The pagoda, which not only gave the place its name but also marks the start of the area known as 'Chinatown', is quite authentic. Made in China, it was shipped here by the city of Fujian Province and donated by Wing Yip and Brothers (Holdings) Ltd.

While many of the underpasses have been filled in and alternatives provided, it is worthwhile looking a second time for the lines of the old paths leading down are clearly visible, particularly in the old design found on the walls.

Ashted Circus and its associated subways only disappeared under a £5.5 million improvement scheme in 2018/19. What is today a crossroads with traffic controlled by traffic lights had for years been a rather unpopular traffic island with a network of subways. The central island, once a green area, was infilled with thousands of tons of earth, the subway tunnel entrances are now bricked up, and the redevelopment has certainly improved the traffic flow along this part of the A4540 Birmingham ring road. Included at the opening ceremony was the burial of a time capsule. Prepared by the pupils of Cromwell Primary School, pupil Roqaya Raik helped bury the capsule, her prize for winning the competition to predict what the junction may look like in the far future. It remains to be seen just when the time capsule will be recovered as it is now buried beneath concrete and tarmac.

Underpasses in the twenty-first century are a comparative rarity compared to the 1950s and 1960s. We will look specifically at that under Old Square later, but there were many more including underpasses at Bristol Street near the former Monaco House, at the Swan in Yardley, Masshouse Circus, Fletcher's Walk at Paradise Circus, Colmore Circus, Five Ways and St Chad's. The latter, part of which has been sealed off, is quite evident as the handrail is still in situ, although today only leads at an angle into the ground.

One pedestrian subway ran from Hill Street to Hurst Street. This was the first in the United Kingdom to be compulsory as the sole means of crossing the road above – if one really does still 'cross' a road from beneath. This formed part of Birmingham's Inner Ring Road around the city centre, the main source of the many underpasses. Intended to be safer for pedestrians, they were soon seen as the haunts of muggers, proved difficult for the

Above: When Jennens Road was built Ashted Bridge was correct but, since widening the road, this is certainly a tunnel.

Left: Underneath does any of Fletcher's Walk still survive?

Looking down to the A45 underpass at the Swan Centre in Yardley. Over the years the bridges have replaced subways, the traffic routes have altered and, as can be seen in the left foreground, pedestrian routes have been blocked off.

elderly to negotiate, and loathed by those with pushchairs or shopping trolleys owing to the ramps to and from street level.

The first section of the Inner Ring Road, and its underpasses, opened in March 1960. The ceremony performed by the newly appointed Minister of Transport, the Rt Hon Ernest Marples MP, who would become infamous for his role in the reshaping of the railways. Often referred to as the Beeching Report, with Dr Richard Beeching's name still universally loathed as a result, it should be Marples name who should be associated with the reports.

Consider, for a moment, the money spent on creating the underpasses and the ring road. In 1960 the first 400-metre section of the ring road opened at a cost of £1,160,000, this out of £15 million budgeted for the entire scheme (the total cost would reach £33 million). Around this time 75 miles of the M1 had opened at a cost of £21 million, equating to £280,000 per mile compared to £5,104,000 per mile for Birmingham's Inner Ring Road. Clearly someone stood to benefit from this expenditure, and the man who held a significant amount of the company producing concrete for these and other road-building schemes (albeit transferred into his wife's name) was Ernest Marples. At least friend Marples did not benefit from the concrete purchased later to block or fill the underpasses.

Few miss the subways, for these were seen as potential danger spots, the haunt of undesirables. Indeed, many would go out of their way to avoid using the tunnels which, when they were built, were supposed to make things safer for users.

Left: Dartmouth Middleway lies beneath the road...

Below: ...and traffic island.

15

ANCHOR EXCHANGE

Named for the link to the Jewellery Quarter, the anchor is the hallmark symbol for the city. This telephone exchange's construction began in 1953. Hiding such a large engineering project just off the city centre would have been impossible, so it was hinted that this was a prelude to Birmingham having its own underground railway system to deflect from the truth.

Opening in September 1957, the work cost £4 million and while supposedly limited to the area around Newhall Street, it certainly spread as far as the Jewellery Quarter and Southside. Over the years updating of the telecommunication systems has been necessary. This included the removal of asbestos used in construction techniques of the time. Firebreaks have been installed and the city's rising water table mean the tunnels are now continually pumped out, although today the tunnels contain only communication cables.

From Telephone House in Newhall Street, it runs south to the Midland Exchange and past to end near the corner of Essex Street and Bromsgrove Street. This was then the BT Stores complex but thereafter redeveloped as flats. Until the tunnels became unsafe some

Above left and above right: Anchor Tunnel. (Image courtesy of BT Heritage & Archives)

Above and below: Anchor Tunnel. (Image courtesy of BT Heritage & Archives)

BT workers would walk along the tunnels between the two buildings to avoid getting wet on rainy days. A planned tunnel to the rear of Hockley Sorting Office never materialised.

During the Cold War, the Anchor Exchange would have been capable of withstanding a nuclear attack, save for a direct hit. As such it doubled as the nuclear bunker for the MPs and councillors of the city, reachable within the standard 'three-minute warning' period. Only put on full alert during the Cuban Missile Crisis, within twenty years much of the equipment was obsolete and slowly emptied. Yet several rooms remain, including the mess and the canteen.

Another tunnel, 2 metres in diameter, is not part of the Anchor but was built over the winter of 1961/62, when the council were developing the ring road and associated constructions. It nears Aston Exchange and the university, stopping at the William Booth Centre in Shadwell Street. The other end passes Telephone House before ending at Broad Street.

Suggestions of how it is possible to walk from the exchange at Smallbrook to its counterpart at Aston Cross are internet myths. For, while cable tunnels do exist, these were never traversable. Similarly, the basement at Aston University has never been connected. Surface evidence can be found at air vents and access points in Fleet Street at Telephone House and the goods lift access in Lionel Street.

Little evidence can be seen from street level today, although the big ventilation ducts around Brindley House and Telephone House are two. Descending from street level via a long metal staircase, two-ton steel doors shut the occupants off from the rest of the world. At lower levels the water problem is apparent for maintenance workers, some 50 metres below the surface, who report hearing the rush of water from even deeper down.

Recently one worker on the excavation spoke of working on excavating the tunnels from 1953. During his four years on the job they excavated four tunnels. Sixty men worked twelve-hour shifts on five days each week, each lowered down 45 metres to their place of work in a bucket, six men at a time. Once underground they remained there until everyone had finished work at the end of the shift. Only men worked the tunnels. Women were employed but only in support positions such as the canteen. They were allowed breaks, but the menu on offer at the canteen proved disappointing. The former employee remembered they only served tomato soup, something he has never been able to stomach since.

One myth to debunk before leaving this impressive construction. Stories are still told of the connection between the tunnels and the Queens Arms in Newhall Street. There is no evidence of any connection with any exterior tunnel or passage in the cellar of the public house. Neither do the known tunnels come close enough to make such possible.

16

REPEATER STATIONS

There were two sites for repeater stations in Birmingham: at Queslett and Lyndon Green. Although firstly, we should clarify just what this is, for most will not have encountered the term. Used in telecommunications, it is an electronic device receiving and rebroadcasting a signal. Such enables the signal to broadcast over longer distances or to get around an obstruction. Such could be used to assist in telephone, television, or radio signals.

Protected repeater stations at Queslett were built between 1951 and 1956. Comprising two levels, with a power source and standby generators, the majority, including this example, were sunken. When operating all this equipment produces heat and ventilation on the upper level proved vital. To protect the equipment heavy blast doors were installed. Conflicting reports suggest either these stations were cleared away when the area was developed or are now buried beneath the modern scene near the junction of Handsworth Drive and the A4041.

Lyndon Green is a telephone repeater station, again installed during the concern associated with the Cold War. It is another with two levels, power source and ventilation system. It is situated on the effective island created by the east and westbound carriageways of the A45 Coventry Road. Built between 1951 and 1956, this sunken station is still in situ and still in use.

Site of the former ROC post at Queslett...

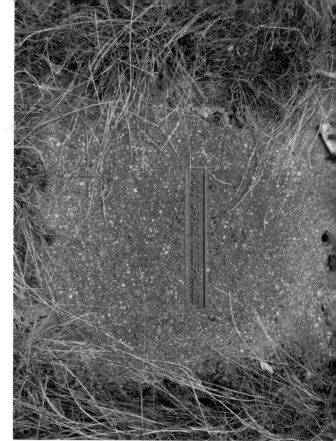

Right: ...and where it was linked to the telephone system.

Below: N. G. Bailey on Coventry Road occupies the site of a repeater station.

17

ROC POST

Royal Observer Corps posts were installed across the country as a warning system for UK defences and designed as a part of the United Kingdom Warning and Monitoring Organisation. Initially manned by British Army personnel, they were followed by Special Constables, and by 1957 by volunteers under the control of the Home Office. A system of 1,563 underground monitoring posts, each 8 miles from the next, provided vital information and data on nuclear detonations. When combined with information from the Meteorological Office, this gave vital information on the clouds of nuclear fallout.

Constructed using reinforced concrete, made waterproof and at least 8 metres deep, they were accessed by a ladder through a shaft to a single room. Here three volunteers had two mattresses, food and water and a generator to keep them alive. Costing £5,000 each, when installed these were a significant investment in the defence of the country and an indication of the perceived danger.

Erdington had just such a monitoring post. Some report it wiped from existence, others point to a post opposite the junction of Reservoir Road and Highcroft Road, but this is inconclusive.

Former ROC post site at Reservoir Road, Erdington.

18

WARSTONE LANE CEMETERY

It may seem obvious to speak of finding a cemetery below ground. Surely all burials are required to be, as the saying goes, '6 feet under'? It came as a huge surprise to discover there is no legal minimum depth for a burial in the United Kingdom, albeit the Ministry of Justice recommends a minimum of 0.6 metres (2 feet) of soil on top of the lid of the coffin to ground level. In practice the average depth is slightly over 1 metre. Often family plots mean two coffins are placed in the same grave, usually at different times, and these are dug to approaching 2 metres.

However, here we are only interested in one cemetery. Warstone Lane in the Jewellery Quarter is home to catacombs. Also known as Brookfields C of E, or the Mint Cemetery, it was established in 1847 to help cope in a massively expanding town (Birmingham was not given city status until 1889). Initially for Anglicans only, other denominations were soon allowed until the last internment in 1982. The last four decades have not been kind to the cemetery. Graves are showing signs of their age, principally as families age themselves and are no longer around to tend them. Recently this deterioration has been addressed by the local authority with pressure from a group of interested individuals and this unique location is slowly being restored.

Our particular interest is in the tiered catacombs. In an ingenious use of a former sand pit, sand extracted for metal casting locally, the two tiers are recessed into the resulting pit. As such it was not a space-saving idea, simply a means of utilising what had already been dug. Once open to the public, the odours proved problematic and the Birmingham Cemeteries Act demanded all coffins not interred directly be sealed with pitch or lead. Now sealed, the catacombs can still be accessed via a path and the inscriptions read.

Right and overleaf above: Warstone Lane cemetery.

The future of the cemetery is hopeful. In 2004 the verbosely named Friends of Key Hill Cemetery and Warstone Lane Cemetery in Birmingham Jewellery Quarter, Hockley, was established. They organise tours on selected days, help maintain the area, and assist in research projects.

Jewellery Quarter Hockley station tunnel.

19

SNOW HILL BRIDGE

To claim this short stretch of the Birmingham and Fazeley Canal as underground will undoubtedly prove controversial. Yet there will be other examples deemed below the surface which, some years earlier, were at (or close to) ground level.

In 1784 parliament approved the construction of the Birmingham and Fazeley Canal. Five years later and its opening linked Birmingham to the Oxford Canal and thus London. Birmingham Snow Hill station – originally Birmingham station, then Great Charles Street station and Livery Street station – opened in October 1852 on the site of what had been Oppenheim's Glassworks. Closing in March 1968, followed by demolition of much of the structure in 1977, was not the end. Since 1987 the newly rebuilt Birmingham Snow Hill station has offered services again. During development work, a significant part of the former glassworks factory and machinery were noted beneath the station site. Since then

Livery Subway under Great Charles Street.

Tunnel from Livery Street underneath the track from Snow Hill.

the area has been designated a site of archaeological importance – very relevant to the theme of this book.

Shortly after leaving the station, trains travelling north out of the city soon cross the canal. As evidenced by the gradient of Livery Street, trains need to descend slowly and a way to span the canal was required. Snow Hill Bridge is an enormous span across a comparatively narrow canal. Constructed using blue bricks, this massive arch is lined by gated arches and interspersed by the occasional work of graffiti. Further along is another lower and more modern bridge alongside a lock and small hut.

A tunnel of huge proportions takes the railway over the canal at Livery Street.

Perhaps the bridge should be regarded as two spans, for just before crossing the canal the tracks cross Lionel Street. At first glance this is a bridge, but its dimensions mean, to the engineer, this is officially defined as a tunnel.

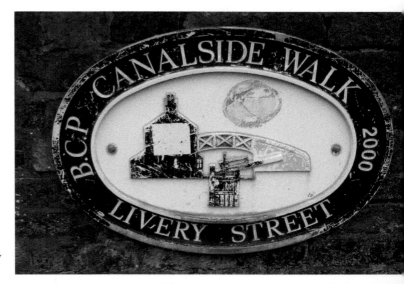

Right: A self-explanatory marker from 2000.

Below: Another view of the canal tunnel at Livery Street.

20

BIRMINGHAM'S WATER SUPPLY

Once every Brummie knew of the Elan Valley and spoke proudly of the engineering marvel bringing fresh water to the 'Second City'. Birmingham's central location, combined with its elevation, means few sources of water are available for any population, doubtless contributing to the slow growth of the eventual city which, at that time, were then seen as separate small settlements. The rapid population expansion in the nineteenth century soon brought about a rise in disease, resulting in Birmingham City Council, led by Joseph Chamberlain, petitioning the government.

Wells had proven increasingly inadequate, with cholera and typhoid epidemics threatening the 650,000 inhabitants. Springs often failed in drier periods. Supplies coming via carts and cans proved inconvenient and unreliable. Wells were sunk at Digbeth, Aston, Witton, Edgbaston, Perry Barr and Kings Vale (now Kingstanding). Well water would later be used primarily by industry. This pumped water was very hard, thus unsuitable for washing and other domestic uses. By the 1830s a supply was gathered from the River Tame near Salford Bridge – a site already examined in chapter 2 – and one of the two reservoirs still visible south of Gravelly Hill Junction; the other is at Edgbaston.

Two 80 bhp engines pumped the water along 76 cm in diameter iron pipes between the two reservoirs. Not only was this almost 4 miles but raised the water over 25 metres from its river source. Leading off these pipes were several fire plugs, providing a source of water for fighting fires and increasing safety considerably. The first supply was ceremoniously drawn in St Paul's Square in March 1831. Hailed as water of exceptional quality, as evidenced by the number of brewers and publicans using it, this soon proved untrue as shown by pollution in the Tame. Indeed, in 1945 pollution levels saw the river declared devoid of life. In recent years this has been reversed and the Tame is now a haven for wildlife.

In 1892 the Birmingham Corporation Water Act allowed the compulsory purchase of all the land within the Elan Valley catchment area. This resulted in some 100 people being forcibly relocated, although only landowners received compensation. Demolition of their homes, three manor houses, a church and a school followed construction of Elan village. Ostensibly built to house the navvies and their families, the locals joined the thousands during the construction of the first four dams, creating five reservoirs: Claerwen, Craig-goch, Pen-y-garreg, Garreg-ddu, and Caban-coch. A new church, Nantgwyllt, can still be seen alongside one dam today.

Opening in 1906, the water comes through valleys, brick tunnels, pipelines and valve houses, only arriving in Birmingham at the very end of its journey. Construction cost £6 million, providing employment for 50,000 for a decade. Carried by aqueduct to

Frankley Reservoir.

Frankley Reservoir, the water, noted for its extreme softness, travels 73 miles entirely by gravity. With a drop of just 52 metres, this means a gradient of just 1:2,300. Travelling at just over 1 mile per hour, a single drop of fresh water takes almost three days to reach Birmingham.

In 1952, in one of her first engagements as monarch, Queen Elizabeth II opened the fifth dam, Claerwen. This came forty-eight years after her great-grandparents, Edward VII and Queen Alexandra, started the water flowing along two 1-metre-diameter pipes. For many years afterwards the Elan Valley proved a popular destination for coach parties from Birmingham. Not until the twenty-first century did Severn Trent Water see a need to find a new source. The dams and aqueducts are now over a century old and in need of maintenance, excellent testimony to the quality of the work. The 15 miles of tunnel and pipeline from the Severn at Lickhill near Stourport were completed in 2018.

Frankley Reservoir holds 900 million litres of water. Until ground-penetrating radar identified the locations of the problem and enabled repairs, leaks accounted for a loss of 540 litres of water each second. Water passes through Frankley Water Treatment Works before users receive it. Any map of the distribution from the reservoir would not only be pointless, as it reaches every home, office, and factory, but (strangely) illegal. Maps of such have been published for maintenance purposes but are considered to be a potential threat to national security.

Left: Model of the Elan Dam…

Below: …in Cannon Hill Park.

21

OLD SQUARE, CORPORATION STREET

Old Square may be Birmingham's best example of a former ground-level feature, now very much subterranean. Today the location seems poorly named as it is clearly not square but an elongated oval. Since 2004 the area has seen all the former underground pedestrian routes raised to the current surface.

Most easily recognised by Bruce Williams' memorial to Birmingham-born Tony Hancock, unveiled 13 May 1996 by Sir Harry Secombe, this was intended to be its temporary site as it was earmarked for New Street. This site was chosen as it stood opposite the blood donor clinic, a reminder of what is probably Hanock's best remembered offering. An earlier design, a mural by Kenneth Budd entitled *Old Square*, appeared in 1967 and still depicts the history of Old Square.

Old Square today…

Left: ...with its old-style sign...

Below: ...and the shopping centre which lay beneath.

Changes in the twenty-first century are only the latest in Old Square's history. Before being filled in, Old Square had been home to a dozen retail outlets. Meats, shoes, magazines, clothing, fruit and vegetables, shoppers could almost fill their entire shopping basket for the week courtesy of the underground shopping centre. While open to the elements, an overhang offered some shelter from inevitable showers. When weather permitted, benches around neatly planted troughs ran along the central area. Accessed via subways from the four roads meeting here, most notably Corporation Street, itself a part of a major development in the late nineteenth century when the roads around here served as a tram junction.

Yet the wholesale changes of the Victorian era merely removed what had become an eyesore. The real square dates from 1713, the focal point between sixteen two-storey Georgian homes. Built as the centrepiece to John Pemberton's Priory Estate, designed by William Westley, the centre was closed off by iron railings with gates permitting access to pedestrian paths. Neglected for some years, in 1832 a public demonstration resulted in stones being thrown – their reaction to the blocking of the Third Reform Bill and denying many of the vote in the forthcoming parliamentary elections.

Earlier still, this had been the Priory of St Thomas of Canterbury, remnants of that time seen in the street names of The Minories, Upper Priory and Lower Priory each allowing access to the hospital. Another, Congreve Street, is where the priory's rabbit warren extended to. Although looking at underground Birmingham here fundamentally looks at the former subway, ironically the underground shopping centre occupied the same level as the priory, itself known as the highest point in Birmingham when constructed. Home to Augustinian canons since at least 1286, records seem to suggest it may have been thriving but had several periods when they failed to meet the conditions imposed in the land gifts. The Dissolution of the Monasteries in 1536 saw the priory abandoned, although the buildings stood until 1547.

Remnants of earlier use were exposed in the Edwardian era. The priory's foundations uncovered during building on The Minories. Large numbers of human bones were uncovered south of Bull Street, thought to have been at least a part of the priory's graveyard. Finally, it seems nothing of the former bomb shelter remains, this dug alongside Lewis's Department Store during the Second World War.

Foundations of the Priory of St Thomas, uncovered during development in the early twentieth century.

Left: The Minories.

Below: The frieze in Old Square tells the history of the area.

22

NATIONAL INDOOR ARENA

The National Indoor Arena, Barclaycard Arena, or whatever sponsorship deal has renamed the thirty-year-old construction at the time of reading, is not strictly where we are looking. As with all of this book we are looking beneath the building. However, the lack of any other signposts means the building will have to suffice as a pointer to what may lie beneath.

In 1846/7 Stephenson took his railway from Birmingham to Wolverhampton, and on to Dudley and terminating at Shrewsbury. Coming into Birmingham New Street station meant, just as today, travelling through a tunnel. Stephenson's tunnel arch has not seen the light since 1989/90 when massive redevelopment of Broad Street was undertaken. This not only included the National Indoor Arena but also Centenary Square, the latter named to mark 100 years since granting Birmingham official city status.

Little information on the length of the tunnel is available today. Rumours abound, including the idea of a station beneath the Arena. If a station ever did exist, the developers failed to notice it or refuse to acknowledge its existence. It seems the tunnel has been either filled in or, more likely, bricked up and will remain out of sight for many years.

23

ASTON HALL

As many would-be historians from Birmingham are always keen to offer, the parish of Aston was long bigger than Birmingham. As with many statistics, this all depends on how each is defined. What is certain is the focal point of Aston is the Grade I listed Jacobean Aston Hall. Built between 1618 and 1635 to a design by John Thorpe, purchasing the house in 1846 meant Birmingham Corporation were the first in Britain to bring a country house to municipal ownership. Today it is a community museum, part of the Birmingham Museums Trust.

Major renovation of the hall, completed in 2009, has seen increased interest in a building that Brummies have always held dear. Perhaps some of those coming here will have heard of the hole made by a cannonball. When Parliamentary troops attacked the house in 1643, it suffered significant damage. For reasons unknown, that caused by the cannonball, which flew through a window and an open door before making a hole in the staircase, has never been repaired. Others will have heard of the tunnel.

While researching this book, several individuals suggested (often more akin to demands) to ensure the Aston Hall Tunnel is included. More than forty years ago the author first heard of a tunnel to Aston Hall, running from the Green Man or Lad in the Lane (depending on which

Aston Hall, the mythical hub of a maze of tunnels...

...one of which is said to lead to the church.

name the Bromford Lane public house was using at the time). There are several problems with this story. Any tunnel would have to be over 2 miles in length. Cut through sandstone would have required shoring up, and wooden supports would require constant maintenance.

The public house stands at an elevation of 106 metres above sea level, Aston Hall at 124 metres. While 18 metres over 2 miles would never be problematic, we need to take into consideration the low point at the Gravelly Hill Junction, this just 91 metres above sea level and now only a mile apart. This severe gradient, and the other slope to the pub, would have created a low point almost directly beneath the confluence of the Rea and the Tame, two of Birmingham's three significant rivers. Running through sandstone, any tunnel here would have been permanently flooded, with no means of pumping the water out prior to the Industrial Revolution and Newcomen's Engine. We can also forget any suggestion of a long descent from Aston Hall to meet a more horizontal tunnel. It does not exist and neither does the entrance at the pub.

But there are other tunnel suggestions. One example is it was an escape route for the Holte family, the only owners of the hall until 1817 and who gave their name to the popular end at Aston Villa Football Club. Some maintain the tunnel could be accessed via trap door under a chair, others point to a large bookcase on a hinge as a secret door.

Some stories say it was sealed to hide the corpse of someone who died from multiple stab wounds. This tunnel, said to run to nearby Aston parish church, a couple of hundred yards away, would not have proven difficult.

The trouble with these stories is they are just stories. There are no tunnels to or from Aston Hall, and there never have been. Including a non-existent tunnel or tunnels may seem, at the very least, inaccurate. Yet the number of leads given to the Aston Hall tunnels demand this myth is put to bed once and for all.

Above: Another tunnel myth…

Left: …at the Lad in the Lane.

24

STRATFORD HOUSE

A Grade II listed building, Stratford House dates from 1601 and was built by Ambrose and Bridget Rotton – their initials are carved over the porch. When built it was the centre of a 20-acre farm. The house has been saved several times. When the London, Midland and Scottish goods yard appeared nearby in 1840, they purchased the building and announced their intention to demolish it. Locals were outraged and this piece of Birmingham history saved.

A century later and, with the house in poor condition, demolition seemed inevitable until Ivon Adams purchased and restored it in 1954. Network Records, leading exponents of techno music, moved in during the eighties and nineties, and little was known of this place until local press published a story in 2015 claiming the latest venture, now known as Tudor Lounge, was a cover for a swingers' club.

Beneath this ancient building is a puzzle. Two short tunnels from the cellar have produced several stories, including an underground route to the town hall. In truth what appears to be two tunnels are likely the remains of a storage facility. In times when keeping produce fresh and cool proved a problem, the obvious answer lay underground. There is no evidence, either physical or written, to show these were ever used for storage, yet there seems no other valid explanation.

25

UNIVERSITY OF BIRMINGHAM MINE

Birmingham has never been considered a mining stronghold. Indeed, it is highly unlikely any profitable mining excavations ever took place within the city's boundaries.

Yet a mine did, and still does, exist. Opened in 1905 in the grounds of the University of Birmingham, the ventilation shafts, covered over, can still be seen near the south gate. It is not deep, the bottom clearly visible when light conditions are favourable. The mine closed in 1960 after five decades in which countless students undertook the course and got to experience underground conditions first-hand.

26

ASHTED CANAL TUNNEL

Heading south along the Grand Union Canal, be it on the water or along the towpath, brings us to Ashted locks and tunnel. The flight of six locks allows us to drop down to the tunnel. This must be the narrowest of Birmingham's canal tunnels. On the water is fine but, walking the towpath, even those of average height should take care not to knock heads against the sloping sides. How a horse would ever have been expected to cope here is a mystery.

At just 94 metres this is not the longest tunnel but certainly an iconic part of Birmingham's extensive canal network. Some may even recall the former Belmont Glassworks standing over the tunnel, and the wharf on exiting which served the Co-operative Society's bakery.

27

CURZON STREET CANAL TUNNEL

Curzon Street is a name better associated with railways. Indeed, the Curzon Street canal tunnel carries no fewer than six lines over the water. At 147 metres, it is sufficiently wide for two boats to pass and includes a tow path with a safety rail. Opened as the Digbeth Branch in 1799, it served many factories and warehouses through several short arms, many of which are still visible, and all considered a part of the Grand Union.

Having already mentioned the railways above, we cannot pass without a mention of the magnificent portal with is Curzon Street station and the terminus of the line to Euston. It is planned to reopen the station as a part of the controversial HS2 link. While archaeology has largely been omitted, here we are concerned mostly with what is not buried and in-filled, it is impossible to ignore a recent discovery. In an area that is earmarked for development as the HS2 terminus, workers have uncovered a turntable. Built by Robert Stephenson, it is thought to date from 1837 when the station first opened. If this is the case it would make it the world's oldest turntable.

Curzon Street's railway turntable, uncovered as part of the redevelopment of the area for HS2.

28

AIR-RAID SHELTERS

Many will recall, either through experience or by reading the history, of the existence of air-raid shelters during the Second World War. We have heard of Anderson shelters, basements, and underground railway constructions being used by people. Everyone is aware that shelters were built after the declaration of war in September 1939. Yet not everything is recorded as it happened, and the truth is very different to what is usually told.

St Martin's Church.

During the four days of the Munich crisis Britain was already preparing. This culminated in Prime Minister Neville Chamberlain returning from negotiations waving the paper and proclaiming 'Peace for our time" – not IN our time as is often quoted. Note the Munich negotiations took place in August 1938, over a year before the declaration of war, and already work on protecting the population of Birmingham was continuing apace.

Already 3 miles of trenches had been dug, enough to accommodate 20,000. By February 1939, a further 10 miles of trenches were planned to be dug. Eventually the trench idea was abandoned, for it provided very little shelter from anything from above. A further 10,000 could use their own basements. These were used, although, at least officially, considered too shallow to provide adequate shelter. An underground car park at St Martin's Tollmarket would house 11,000 during an air raid, with other sites considered for the city centre.

All these public shelters soon proved inadequate. When bombing started in August 1940 more than half the Anderson shelters were abandoned in favour of public shelters. Despite being summertime, half the underground Anderson shelters were already flooded. This meant 20,000 were moving to public shelters, overcrowded conditions soon proving a health risk for they were in almost constant use for the next two years, albeit raids were sporadic after April 1941.

The author was delighted to hear from Gary O'Brien, who pointed out an air-raid shelter that is still underground. On Marsh Lane, Erdington and directly opposite Hammond Drive, there is a grassy hump where, on the one side, steps lead down to a locked iron gate, which once gave access to the air-raid shelter here.

Air-raid shelter in Erdington.

29

ARCHAEOLOGY

Having mentioned archaeology at Curzon Street, we should also briefly mention other such sites in the city. Note this is not intended to be comprehensive and could never claim to be so, for who could categorically announce there was nothing more to be found in the ground?

Weoley Castle is a fortified manor house. Dating from the thirteenth century and home to the Dudley family, what remains are the lower walls, but we should also realise there is at least as much unseen in the foundations.

Metchley Fort is a former Roman station on Icknield Street. The site is now occupied by Queen Elizabeth Hospital. Archaeologists estimate it dates from AD 70, just twenty-seven years after the Romans arrived in Britain, but had been abandoned by AD 120.

Kent's Moat is a moated medieval site in Yardley dating from the twelfth century. To find an excavation of such an age so well defined is remarkable and a testament to how well this conservation area has been maintained.

Gannow Green is another moated site. Here evidence of walls and hearths suggest several phases of occupation between the thirteenth and fifteenth centuries.

Weoley Castle.

Above: Metchley
Fort near
Queen Elizabeth
Hospital and
the Birmingham
University…

Left: …a
former Roman
stronghold.

Below: As the
sign says, Kent's
Moat…

THE HAYS KENT'S
26   MOAT

…although somewhat overgrown these days.

Construction of the M6 Toll Motorway saw remains of Bronze Age, Iron Age and Roman remains uncovered near Langley Mill Farm off Lindridge Road.

Fox Hollies Park contains a Bronze Age burnt mound. Horseshoe-shaped and very overgrown, it has never been excavated but geophysical surveys suggest there are at least seven distinct pits, which are separated by significant amounts of stone.

Cob Lane in Bourneville is home to another burnt mound. This example was excavated in 1980/81, although it did not enable archaeologists to agree whether these were used purely for cooking or as saunas. What is agreed is their longevity, carbon dating showing this was in use between 2,800 and 3,700 years ago.

Little remains of the moat at Gannow Green.

Floodgate Street, Digbeth, saw archaeologists called in August 2001 to examine the site prior to development. Two trenches revealed nineteenth-century cellars intruding on medieval remains, even utilising the same sandstone blocks as footings in both eras.

Parsonage Moat, near the junction of Edgbaston Street and Pershore Street, is thought to have been an original twelfth-century construction, which was later developed as a manor house around the fourteenth century. It gets its name from its subsequent rebuild as the parsonage for St Martin's in the Bull Ring. No trace remains as it lies under the Bull Ring's markets.

Above: The M6 Toll Road took away the archaeology.

Below: Fox Hollies Park.

30

LAPAL TUNNEL

A narrow brick-lined tunnel built in 1798 by the aptly named William Underhill. At 3,740 metres and with no towpath, legging this tunnel would have proven exhausting work. With a width of 2.36 metres, this just 22 cm wider than the maximum width of the boats using it, and with a clearance of 1.8 metres, it would not have been a journey for the claustrophobic.

Running beneath Lapal, Woodgate Country Park, and close to junction 3 of the M5, the tunnel suffered many collapses until 1917 when the final collapse saw the canal abandoned. Some sections of the canal have been filled in while other stretches are dry.

With the resurgence of interest in canals, in 1990 the Lapal Canal Trust were formed with the hope of reopening the canal and tunnel to traffic. Seventeen years later a study showed the restoration of the tunnel would be prohibitive. Since then the trust have amended their target to restore the canal to come through the Woodgate Valley by an 'over the top' route.

Some indication of the size of this engineering marvel is seen in the idea of how, more than two centuries later, it is more feasible to spend £1.2 million to create a new canal with locks than reopen an existing tunnel. Until the project is completed, the line of the tunnel can be followed over the top by a series of mounds, former ventilation shafts.

31

SOHO HOUSE

From 1766 to 1809 Matthew Boulton, one of the leading lights of early industry, lived at what is now known as Soho House. A pioneer of mass production using the production line, Boulton, his colleagues, and his contemporaries founded the Lunar Society. Meeting here from 1789, Boulton and his descendants made many changes to the design of the house. After several changes of ownership, including as a hostel for police officers, the building came to Birmingham City Council in 1990 who, in 1995, opened this as a museum.

The Soho Manufactory, established in 1761, initially made use of power provided by a water mill. Quickly a steam engine enabled water to be pumped back to run through the wheel again. By 1788 the steam engine powered the factory directly, producing a range of metal products. The factory ran until 1860, after which the land was utilised for smaller factories and houses.

Years later, during restoration of Soho House, excavations revealed a pit near the front wall foundations and its cellar. Here copper coin blanks and a Sumatran coin dated 1803 suggest this was where such were minted. Further evidence comes in the shape of the tunnel, now bricked up, which we know once held a drive shaft. Constructed in 1824/6, the tunnel has been traced at other points and linked to a second tunnel at right angles, which leads to where we know the steam engine was sited.

Soho House.

32

TOILETS

Some may recall the underground toilets of the city centre. Two gentleman's facilities come to mind, each long gone and yet both are still rumoured to be in situ. One of these occupied the junction of Stephenson Street and New Street, outside the Midland Hotel. It is thought this disappeared in the 1970s.

The second example stood on the other side of the tracks, south of New Street station. Some have commented on the comparatively wide mouth of the junction of Hill Street and Station Street. Here, on the island at the mouth of the road now occupied by an advertising column, once stood the second underground toilet.

In both cases steps led down to what had been a Victorian installation, with delightful tiling and oak doors to cubicles. At one time these were manned during opening hours, kept spotlessly clean and something the city could be proud of. Unfortunately, when New Street underwent regeneration in the sixties, the toilets were not included. Station Street's example had disappeared by 1970 and Stephenson Street ten years later.

Underground toilet at the corner of Hill Street and Station Street. (Courtesy of Warwickshire Railways)

33

BROAD STREET

Broad Street has so much running beneath road level, it could almost qualify as a flyover. We could easily have covered at least three quite separate access tunnels here, but that would have proven an inadequate reflection of the different levels found beneath road and pavement level in Broad Street.

We must start with that which is easily the most visible. Looking at Gas Street Basin from where the canal passes beneath Broad Street enables us to get our bearings. Note the tunnel under here is officially listed as No. 266 Broad Street and both the building and the tunnel are listed buildings. From here look directly east and the tallest building this side of Suffolk Queensway. The tower is approximately where the railway track forming part of the cross-city route runs beneath. Here we get some indication of the various levels, as Suffolk Queensway disappears beneath Paradise Circus as the Queensway Tunnel, but passes over the railway line.

The track makes a turn to the left and passes south of the building housing the Consulate General of the Islamic Republic of Pakistan. Here we can glimpse the dual track as it emerges into the light for some 50 metres parallel to Holliday Street opposite the junction with Bridge Street. It is difficult to see the track, especially from the street, as the wall and the depth of the track bed work against us and block the view.

An indication of the track's depth can be gauged from how the line quickly passes under the canal at the section known as Birmingham Canal Old Line. The canal takes a sharp

Broad Street runs over the top but underneath. This certainly qualifies as a tunnel.

left turn shortly afterwards and parallels the now hidden railway for some miles. Daylight can be seen on the tracks again at Granville Street, but for little more than 100 metres before another tunnel. Emerging after Bath Row and under the tunnel carrying Lee Bank Middleway, we find the station at Five Ways.

Looking from the bridge above Five Ways station, or even the steps leading to and from the platforms, we can see how closely the railway and canal follow the same course. Note the canal has no locks on this stretch for some considerable distance and thus perfectly level. Trains dislike gradients and having recently passed under the canal is still significantly below canal level.

We will return to this line in a later chapter, but here it is worthwhile pausing and returning to the canal to dispel an oft-told myth. From our starting point, on the bridge over the canal in Broad Street, we are going to cross over the look the opposite way towards the National Sea Life Centre and the Old Turn Junction. Here the most obvious permanent canal feature is the island in the middle of the junction, which, according to many, is an airshaft leading to the railway tunnel below the canal.

Thanks to Andrew Tidy, and many maps of this area from over the years, I can dispel this idea. For a start there are plenty of other places to site an airshaft. More importantly, this supposed shaft does not sit above a railway line, at least not a modern one. To have sited a potential accident site and the chance of millions of litres of canal water pouring through an airshaft when the inevitable accident happened would be madness. Narrowboats hitting obstructions were not simply commonplace, but seemingly an inevitability, if newspaper reports are anything to go by.

But the clearest evidence that this is not an airshaft comes from maps. Compare every map you can find, and it is soon evident this 'island' has moved many times during its existence. While we should always make allowances for errors by cartographers, there are simply too many variables to make this an airshaft.

Before leaving Broad Street and canal network, we shall take a short detour in the company of Colin Sidaway. On one of his travels along the Newhall Branch, near to what Brummies refer to as the Longboat Pub, Colin found a tunnel running underground and had included a lock that dropped down into Baskerville Basin off Broad Street. This is almost certainly the stretch labelled Gibson Arm on an old sketch map dating from the early twentieth century. Cut in the grounds of Easy Hill House, John Baskerville's home, the lock is Gibson's Lock. It seems it is impossible to locate unless on the water.

The canal version of a traffic island, never a ventilation shaft.

34

ELMDON AIRPORT BUNKER

When researching, the author very quickly realised examples in Birmingham fell into two categories. Many routes burrow under heavily built-up areas, the reason clearly to avoid adding to traffic above ground and finding a trouble-free route below. It also means there is little likelihood of future disruptions to the route through such as roadworks, weather, traffic lights or pedestrian crossings.

We also have those in more rural locations, often closer to the boundaries of the town or city. That these are still in situ is down to the simple fact that the land has never been required for other uses. Thus, many are abandoned and most either locked or sealed to ensure there is no danger of anyone becoming trapped or injured there. An example of the latter is found on land now occupied by Birmingham International Airport, formerly

Above left: Concrete slabs on Elmdon's former bunker... (Image courtesy of Midge)

Above right: ...the entrance leading to... (Image courtesy of Midge)

...the rather gloomy interior. (Image courtesy of Midge)

known as Elmdon Airport, and the author is indebted to Midge for the information and the photographs.

During the Second World War Elmdon served as a military airfield from 1939. A location so far from potential enemy targets made this site ideal for use as a training facility and this was the base for the Elementary Flying Training School 51 Group. While those here did not see much in the way of offensive action, its location close to the giant industrial city meant it would often be targeted by enemy bombing raids. Whether civilian or military, shelters were provided to keep them safe during these raids and one such shelter was built at Elmdon. That bomb shelter still exists.

Two intersecting runways with several aircraft hangars served Elmdon Airport until extensions to the north and west formed part of the change to this becoming Birmingham Airport. Built in 1941, the bomb shelter, officially designated Battle Headquarters, is of concrete construction and from here the airfield's defence would have been organised in the event of enemy attack. Consisting of three rooms, with a connecting corridor, stairs allowed access from one side and a ladder leading to the roof.

Time has not been kind to this wartime relic. Vandals have taken their toll but not as much as nature. Regular flooding, with fluctuating water levels up to 2 metres deep, has brought in soil and rubbish, making exploration impossible.

With the changes over the years to the A45 or Coventry Road, as well as the airport, the bunker is no longer an obvious part of the modern airport. However, on the opposite side of the new section of the A45 a small group of trees hide this relic from the Second World War. It would not be advisable to descend into the bunker – it is not safe.

35

LEWIS'S IN CORPORATION STREET

The former Lewis's store in Corporation Street may be linked to the following chapter on the Old Square and Priory Square. Although there is a clear link in the vicinity above ground, it is difficult to visualise how these would be linked beneath the surface. Note it is correct to refer to it as Lewis's and not John Lewis, for when the store was open in Birmingham, the retail outlet was known as such.

Evidence for the connection came in the form of a couple of reports from yesteryear, when Lewis's stood proudly as one of three or four retailers where Birmingham's shoppers could purchase anything and everything for the family or the home. Yet these earlier reports speak of nothing specific, and there is no reason why they should, when the only means of bringing goods into the store would have been through the basement access.

Yet years later, with that means of access long forgotten and the department store having vacated the building above, news leaked out of this being utilised to store Christmas trees earmarked for Priory Square. Research failed to reveal the original source and nothing

Another view of Old Square from the nineteenth century.

Priory Square service road is still in existence underground...

...and the difference in the modern road level compared to the actual ground level is shown here.

definitive could be found to substantiate whether some of Birmingham's city centre trees had waited here prior to going on display among the lights and shoppers. This does not mean there is no truth in the tale, simply it could not be confirmed.

Two versions of the story can be found. While this does cast some doubt on its authenticity, it does not mean both are not worth telling. Both agree on the storage of the conifers and both speak of a storage room designated 'Number 2'. While one speaks of rusting railway lines being found behind a shuttered door, the second version speaks of the goods arriving by lorry. Either way this means a significant hollow underneath the building, not just a basement but a space with a good height to permit vehicles to come along here.

If the access came in the form of a railway track, it is not difficult to envisage a siding running from the line now used by trains between Snow Hill and Moor Street and passing beneath the Great Western Arcade. Yet it is not too long since people walked this half-mile tunnel and nobody reported or recorded an access tunnel heading north, although such was noticed heading south as is mentioned in Chapter 3. The author suspects this is a case of two stories being intertwined and Christmas trees arrived by road.

This does not explain how the trees arrived here but there is a very likely explanation which is still evident to this day. All will be revealed in the following chapter. Yet before we leave Lewis's we must remember the Second World War. To offer the people of Birmingham a place of refuge during the many bombing raids, a large hole was dug alongside the store and a bomb shelter constructed within. Many lives were saved by this shelter, which lived a charmed life and avoided the direct hit that would have killed those inside had one of the bombs been on target. There is no evidence of the shelter today.

Above: Great Western Arcade from the top end.

Left: Inside the Great Western Arcade.

36

PRIORY SQUARE

To continue from the previous chapter and the story of the former Lewis's store, it will seem unlikely that Priory Square and a basement in Corporation Street could be linked. While distance is hardly prohibitive, only 150 metres separate them, it is not difficult to see that Priory Square is among the highest ground floor points in the city centre. Except this is not ground level.

Here is an opportunity to see just how much the Second City has raised street level over the decades. Stand on the south side of Priory Queensway and look down from the bridge to Dale End. The road below is as close to true ground level as we can get in this area. Below and to the right is an access point, an opening where vehicles are able and do drive beneath the buildings and one which is no mystery. We know where it goes and its purpose as the sign tells us, for it reads 'PRIORY SQUARE SHOPPING CENTRE SERVICE ROAD'. Note this is the exit point – the entrance is about 50 metres further along.

It does not take an architectural expert to realise this is no twenty-first-century construction. This has been here since Priory Square was developed more than fifty years ago. If this route enables goods to be brought into the many retail outlets above, it is equally possible that an earlier, and possibly still current, access tunnel reaches to the old basement of John Lewis.

Note the two mentions of a 'priory' in modern street names. This link can be traced through Birmingham's records and maps to two earlier phases of construction in 1897 and 1797. In the nineteenth century the recently cut Corporation Street ran very much along its present course. As shown in the illustration, Priory Queensway has replaced two streets, Upper Priory and Lower Priory, while two others have been retained. The mall known as the Minories is another reminder of the former religious community – of which more in a moment – and what is now known as Old Square feature in the eighteenth century, although they would have looked very different indeed.

Old Square may seem a misnomer, for clearly the region is either oval or circular, depending upon which era we examine. Today pedestrians walk at the same level as the traffic. Yet as recently as the end of the last century a whole shopping community existed beneath here. Linked by subways under Priory Queensway and open to the sky in the centre, shoppers emerged to a mini-shopping centre with units housing a butcher, greengrocer and fruiterer, a shoe shop, clothes, a mini-mart and, throughout its entire life, a newsagent and tobacconist. Today this is all buried beneath the slabs of Old Square.

Yet even this does not take us back anywhere near the beginning of the story. The retail units were only installed in the 1950s and 1960s. The Square is, as the name suggests, much older. Just when the Priory of St Thomas of Canterbury began is unclear, but there are records of what seems a well-established community in 1286. Foundations of the priory were uncovered in the nineteenth century when builders were working on the Minories.

Dissolved in 1536, the structures were demolished eleven years later, but the site rumbled on, albeit greatly reduced in size and numbers, until purchased by John Pemberton in 1697. Rather than repair, Pemberton further levelled the site to build the Priory Estate. It is the square that interests us. This dates from 1713, when bordered by sixteen two-storey houses in the Georgian style designed by William Westley. His print is reproduced here.

Note the central portion of the square. Fenced off by iron railings, the central focus where several footpaths met. Again, the square fell into neglect and little is heard until 1832 when a public demonstration erupted here. Trees and railings were removed by 1837, allowing traffic to come through here. But the region proved too narrow for the vehicles and for this reason Birmingham Street Commissioners widened and eventually redeveloped the roads by 1897.

As we can see, the real ground level in Birmingham is some way below where pedestrians walk today. Odd to think that the former shops beneath Old Square would be at ground level in the city's history.

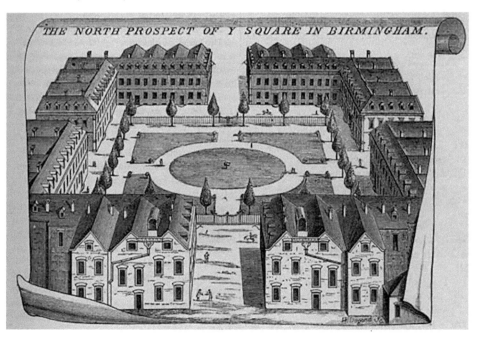

Woodcut of the Old Square from 1732.

37

BIRMINGHAM INTERNATIONAL STATION

Tunnels are rarely as accessible as this, albeit that access is denied for most of the time, which conversely means it is very easy to find. Emerging from the main entrance of the station, turn left and follow the road for 100 metres. There, on the left-hand side, reached by steps or a ramp, is a 25-metre tunnel.

This tunnel allows access for visitors to and from the National Exhibition Centre, specifically the Genting Arena and Resorts World, to come under the tracks and reach the station. With padlocked gates on either end it never looks particularly inviting unless allowing access when, we would hope, the accumulated water and wind-blown detritus will have been removed.

Underpass between Birmingham International station and the NEC.

38

THE BONES OF ST MARTIN'S

In 2020, archaeologists excavating sites in Birmingham prior to the laying of the high-speed rail link known as HS2 reported on their findings of burials uncovered in Park Street. Considering the subject matter of this book, the ultimate irony of the controversial line, most often objected to as it would spoil scenery or bisect areas, could be largely avoided were HS2 to run entirely through one long tunnel. Such a solution would also add a contemporary chapter to *Going Underground: Birmingham*.

While many think the St Martin's Church depicted on paintings of the city still stands, the present building only dates from 1873 and replaced the earlier version completed by 1263. During cleaning work in the early twenty-first century, archaeologists were called in to assist in identifying and cataloguing everything before cleaning, removal, or relocation.

The remains which interest us lie in the crypt, a remnant of the earlier church that had been incorporated in the new building. Although burial records for here begin in 1554, bodies were certainly interred in the former graveyard much earlier than the sixteenth century. By the late eighteenth century, the number of burials here had raised the level of the churchyard. An amusing comment from the pen of William Hutton in 1783 pointed out how the churchyard incorporated so much 'refuse of life' it was becoming a hill and before long the growth of the soil would see the dead burying the church, rather than the reverse.

St Martin's closed its graveyard in 1848, the same year as the forementioned Park Street opened for burials, although family graves accepted burials until 1915. In 1974, Birmingham Museum staff were invited to excavate the crypt. Their investigations revealed a vault two-thirds full of disarticulated human skeletal remains. Church representatives stress they were removed shortly afterwards but what happened to them is unclear.

Some sources insist they were cremated, while others recall them being reburied, with Witton Cemetery being cited as their final resting place. Neither explanation seems particularly satisfactory. Burying the remains en masse elsewhere may seem the logical answer – they had been interred this way for many years and returning them to that state sounds sensible. However, this would require a rather different understanding from Birmingham City Council, the cemetery's owners, and the agreement of any relatives. The relatives may also object to cremation for, while it is commonplace today, the first official cremation in the United Kingdom did not happen until 26 March 1885.

Yet, for inclusion in the book the item simply needs to be underground and the crypt is still in situ.

39

CAR PARKING

After first passing our driving test and going out on our own for the first time, one of the most daunting experiences is to park the car in the parking area. This is particularly arduous when having to negotiate the ramps associated with a multistorey car park. In recent years multistoreys are increasingly more likely to reach down rather than up. Most certainly an aesthetic improvement, but equally daunting for the new driver and far scarier for the claustrophobic.

For Brummies the city centre has half a dozen underground or partially underground car parks, although there are other private underground car parks associated with hotels and office buildings. Both the purpose-built Cube and the Mailbox have been open for more than a decade, while the B4 and Grand Central car parks are adapted from earlier constructions.

Of all of these it is that descending into the ground from Smallbrook Queensway, suitably known as the Bullring Parking, taking drivers down the ramp into the bowels of Birmingham. Or at least that is how it feels, and yet where we are really heading is under the raised street level of late twentieth-century Brum and into an area which any regular travellers to the city will have seen and doubtless used at some point. Here we are in what was referred to as the Midland Red Bus Station, which stood alongside Birmingham's famous indoor market and brought untold millions to shops and workplaces for many years.

The Mailbox car park.

Some will remember it as where passengers could await the arrival of their bus undercover and away from the inclement and unpredictable British weather. Yet most will recall the noise and fumes from the many diesel engine vehicles.

Above: When the Bullring was still the Bull Ring. (Courtesy of Hammerson)

Below: Bullring underground parking.

40

SELLY OAK'S MYSTERY

An appeal for underground locations in the Birmingham press resulted in a few offerings. Some of these I had already discovered, while others were duplications, but a few did bring about new leads, and all of these have been included. To all those who responded, a big thank you. Yet there was one story which came from a gentleman who wished to remain anonymous. It came to him second hand and neither he nor the author were able to check the validity of the claim. However, the chance it may exist means it has to be given space.

This gentleman spoke of a friend who had been called to repair the wall of a tunnel or bridge. When travelling south from Five Ways, the repair was required in the tunnel wall shortly before Selly Oak station. When the repair team arrived on the scene, they discovered a hole in the wall. It is claimed they realised a huge vault existed behind the wall and, when shining a light through the hole, the team were staring at a huge storage facility housing any number of military vehicles. It is said these are kept here awaiting mobilisation in the event of a major threat to the nation.

Looking at the line there are several bridges between Five Ways and Selly Oak stations, but only one tunnel. That tunnel runs under Church Street, Edgbaston, near its junction

Selly Oak station…

...but no sign of a cache of anything today.

with Carpenter Road and could possibly have something hiding beneath it. It should be noted the story states before Selly Oak and this site is, geographically, clearly closer to Five Ways. Bridges with a brick wall cross the track at St James Road, where the canal and houses mean nothing could exist alongside; at Somerset Road, where similar problems discount this site; at Pritchatts Road, where there is a small space on one side, away from the adjacent canal; at University where Westgate crosses and there is an opportunity for something below the station car park; and after Selly Oak station the line runs along an embankment and there are no tunnels nearby.

Does the storage facility exist? Is it an urban legend, one man's fantasy, or did the source get the location wrong? It would be an exciting thought to think such existed below the streets of Birmingham and ready to defend us in our hour of need, but with the information available, it does not seem possible that such exists. Unless the reader knows differently, of course.

41

KINGS NORTON CANAL TUNNEL

An important and significant tunnel and one which is both a part and not a part of Birmingham at the same time. Correctly known as Wast Hills Tunnel, this 2,492-metre tunnel opened to traffic in 1796. There are signs of the tunnel above ground in the form of the ventilation shafts, initially created for ventilation during construction – after opening the flow of air through the tunnel provides more movement of air than the shafts. Yet the shafts do show the course of the tunnel beneath Wast Hills.

The confusion as to whether it is a part of Birmingham is because it begins within the city's boundaries but emerges to the south outside the city. Indeed, not only is it outside the city but also in a different county. The northern opening is at Hawkesley in Birmingham, while the southern end is in Worcestershire. Note while there is ample room for two boats to pass in opposite directions, this tunnel has never had a towpath.

This canal tunnel is very straight and thus while we would expect to see light from the exit at the other end, this very much depends upon atmospheric conditions. Humidity will blur visibility, and there is certainly enough water to raise humidity, thus it depends on the movement of air through the tunnel as to whether we can make out the exit.

42

UNDER THE BULL RING

Considering the author's interest in etymology, hence his many books on place names, the Bull Ring should not be discussed before considering its name. For the younger generation, this famous area of the city is the Bullring. Prior to redevelopment at the turn of the twenty-first century, and for at least six centuries, this had been the Bull Ring. This referred to the green in the Corn Cheaping (Market) where bulls were chained for bull-baiting. Chains linked the ring in the bull's nose, but the name refers to the iron ring at the other end of the chain.

Is Bullring correct? Or Bull Ring? The original form is the correct spelling for the ring in the creature's nose, but there is no precedent for the form to describe the ring on the post. For Brummies the Bull Ring would have been the name of the shopping centre as depicted on the outside of the previous incarnation, complete with a silhouette of a bull, and that was seen as the name of this shopping experience. When the new version appeared as Bullring, many sought to reinstate the 'traditional spelling', when the owners clearly considered it a name and one known by a single word.

As the Bull Ring/Bullring has undergone several redevelopments over the years, it will be interesting to see whether future changes will see the name appear as one or two words. Whichever is chosen it will not surpass the revelation the last time work went on here from 1999. A ditch was discovered, a boundary footpath separating houses from a deer park.

Among the accumulated rubbish preserved, such is always a big clue to earlier usage and an excellent dating tool for archaeologists, were fragments of pottery and evidence of leather tanning. This may not seem much to the uninitiated, but pottery styles change quite rapidly over time and with the right tools, it is possible to discover what the pot once held. Similarly, the tanning process, albeit largely unchanged for centuries, did benefit from improved methods over time and thus provides further clues.

Two decades ago, the discovery of a lost street/path raised many eyebrows. How could an entire way be lost? It did seem very much a unique find for Birmingham's city centre. Yet in 2019 work on extending West Midlands Metro revealed another former footpath near Victoria Square and Pinfold Street. The clay pipe, pottery and metal items were removed and eventually put on show in Birmingham Museum and Art Gallery.

Hence inside twenty years a unique find had suddenly become twice as common. It then raised the question as to how many other streets, lanes and footpaths have disappeared from Birmingham's maps. Only time, excavation, and a great deal of work will tell.

43

ICEHOUSES

In times before refrigeration became commonplace, only the larger houses with their bigger budget could afford a cooling system for foodstuffs in the warmer months. Known as icehouses, these would be buried underground to reduce the chance of ambient heat warming the storage chamber while also insulating the facility. Storing a large amount of ice in a small and sealed room will keep the ice from melting quickly for weeks. The same is true today for freezers – a modern freezer filled with food is far more efficient than one nearly empty, for cold air warms much quicker and escapes from the container every time it is opened.

In Birmingham, the icehouses of two old homes are still in situ, albeit not in use for many years. An icehouse did the same job as a refrigerator, with perhaps 20 tons of ice filling the compartment when it is first filled. Food and other perishables would be stored on or among the blocks of ice, the doors kept shut unless gaining access.

Icehouses, of which some 3,000 were thought to have existed, were installed in the homes of the rich and influential from the middle of the eighteenth century until near the end of the

Moseley Hall's former icehouse in what is now a private park.

nineteenth century. Some were in use until before the Second World War, but the invention of the refrigerator and the decline of large country houses made these storage facilities obsolete.

Moseley Park's icehouse can be found south of the pathway and past the tennis pavilion. A Grade II listed building, it is opened on special days for pre-booked visitors. Staff at Moseley Hall would collect ice from the lake and snow when it fell deep enough in barrows and pack it into the icehouse during the winter. Archaeologists have identified a brick pathway laid solely for the transportation of the ice to the icehouse. Within, the entrance leads to a sharp right-angle turn, another trick to minimise admitting warmer air to the 3-metre-wide and 4.2-metre-high chamber when opened during the summer. Straw, sacking and other insulating materials would be used to cover the frozen water to further increase the length of time the temperature stayed low enough to keep the ice solid. Thanks to Moseley Society, Moseley Hall's former icehouse was saved by an appeal for funds at the end of the twentieth century.

A second icehouse can still be found on the site of the former Hamstead Hall, near Acfold Road in Handsworth. Not the original hall that stood near the junction of Hamstead Hall Avenue and Beauchamp Avenue, this new mansion was constructed in the early eighteenth century but only stood until 1935, when it was all but demolished. Part of the walled garden remains in woodland to the rear of Greenway and Croftway, with the ruined icehouse near the River Tame. Built about 1776, the chamber here is also 3 metres in diameter and originally its domed roof reached 4.3 metres in height. This depth had been achieved by digging down a little over 2 metres below the level of entrance passageway.

The River Tame alongside the former icehouse belonging to Hamstead Hall.

44

PICCADILLY ARCADE

In 1910 the Piccadilly Cinema opened in Birmingham. Advertised as a luxury cinema, it remained open for just sixteen years. Its short life had nothing to do with lack of customers; indeed it proved so popular a second cinema was built to accommodate the numbers. Meanwhile this site became Piccadilly Arcade. Leading from New Street to Stephenson Place, the natural slope of the land lends itself well to the contours of a cinema. Yet what interests us here is what lies underneath the arcade.

As Gary O'Brien pointed out, recently a select group were allowed into the subterranean area. Here they saw reminders of the decorative plasterwork of the cinema. Portcullis and fleur de lys designs on the walls were interspersed with inexplicable numbers and tally marks. Unexplained, that is, until someone pointed out at one time this had been home to a snooker hall.

Piccadilly Arcade and, looking above, signs of the former use is evident.

45

FINAL THOUGHTS

As we have seen, the idea of solid ground beneath our feet is a myth. Sewers, passages, tunnels, cables, pipes, excavations, underpasses, drains, mine workings, underground rivers, and much more honeycomb that supposed terra firma.

This book has only looked at man-made examples. What if we were to add that produced by animals, other than Homo sapiens, and the tunnels created by the myriad creatures which share our planet and constantly drive through the soil, the picture becomes even bigger. A worm may not be large but there are thousands of them. In what a gardener would describe as 'good earth' there are at least a thousand in every square metre. Moles, rabbits, badgers, assorted rodents, and a myriad insect species burrow through the ground. It does make us wonder how much ground there is left to dig through.

Remains of the Bull Street and Corporation Street underpass.

Such images become so mind-boggling they are difficult to visualise, if not impossible. Hence, let us look at any street. It does not matter which for everywhere has a similar collection of tubes and wires beneath the pavements and roads. Take a short road, just thirty properties in length. Cables for electricity, telephones and television (including internet), gas, fresh water, domestic wastewater, flushed waste from toilets, and drains from the gutter all means the first couple of metres under the street are nowhere near 100 per cent earth.

What is more that extends along the whole thirty properties. That is about 150 metres in length and remember we are only talking about one side of the street. Also, that applies no matter if we are looking at a row of tenement houses from the nineteenth century, or a lavish spread of multi-bedroomed detached properties with good-sized gardens. The size of the properties is irrelevant, the pipes and cables have still to reach each property.

Next time you see the road dug up, maybe as you walk past, take a quick peep into the hole. You will likely get some odd looks, but you will not a care as you are fascinated by the complexity of something you walk over with every single step, albeit unseen. No wonder the road has to be dug up for maintenance purposes and thank goodness that collection of cables and pipes is not above ground. There would be very little room left for us.

BIBLIOGRAPHY

Bartlam, Norman, *Broad Street, Birmingham*
Bird, Vivian, *Portrait of Birmingham*
Birmingham City Council, *Developing Birmingham 1889 to 1989*
Buteux, Simon, *Beneath the Bull Ring*
Harvey, David, *Birmingham Past and Present: The City Centre Volume 1*
Hodder, Michael, *Birmingham: The Hidden History*
Skipp, Victor, *The Making of Victorian Birmingham*
Sutcliffe, Dr. A. R., *Provision of Air Raid Shelters in Birmingham During the Second World War*
Whybrow, John, *How Does Your Birmingham Grow?*